The Hunter's Handbook

Endgame's Guide to Adversary Hunting

Karen Scarfone, CISSP, ISSAP

Foreword by Jamie Butler

CYBEREDGE
PRESS

The Hunter's Handbook—Endgame's Guide to Adversary Hunting

Published by:
CyberEdge Group, LLC
1997 Annapolis Exchange Parkway
Suite 300
Annapolis, MD 21401
(800) 327-8711
www.cyber-edge.com

For general information on CyberEdge Group research and marketing consulting services, or to create a custom *Definitive Guide* book for your organization, contact our sales department at 800-327-8711 or info@cyber-edge.com.

ISBN: 978-0-9961827-2-0 (paperback); ISBN: 978-0-9961827-3-7 (eBook)

Printed in the United States of America.

10 9 8 7 6 5 4 3 2 1

Publisher's Acknowledgements

CyberEdge Group thanks the following individuals for their respective contributions:

Editor: Susan Shuttleworth
Designer: Debbi Stocco
Publishing Coordinator: Steve Piper

Table of Contents

Foreword

As new data breaches surpass previous breaches in size and scope, it's clear that perimeter firewalls and antivirus detection are inadequate for today's threat environment. Cyberespionage and cybercrime have proliferated, with attackers bypassing defenses at will to steal unprecedented amounts of intellectual property and personally identifiable information. Even small companies are becoming targets for their IP and as a means to access partner or customer companies within a supply chain. Clearly, the status quo is broken.

We all recognize that incidents are inevitable. Now, how do we act on this knowledge? What can we do differently to prevent a breach? The industry requires a new approach that's as dynamic as these threats and the enterprise environments they target. Organizations are seeking ways to get "left of boom" by detecting and blocking adversaries *before* damage occurs. Looking in the rearview mirror and responding after the fact are no longer adequate.

Unfortunately, security solutions haven't advanced at the same pace as adversaries. The industry continues to apply new names to obsolete solutions, embellishing the terminology while the technology remains stuck in time. *Hunt* remains almost as ill-defined as other buzzwords – big data, cloud, APT, etc. Hunt is frequently confused with indicator search capabilities or glorified log sorting. This misunderstanding fails to capture the full promise of a hunt approach.

We see hunting as an essential component of security. It is the *proactive, stealthy, and surgical* detection and eviction of adversaries inside your network without known indicators of compromise. Hunting is an offense-based strategy; hunting is thinking like the attacker. If you were the adversary, what would you attack, for what purpose, and how? Attackers have a mission. Hunting must be able to derail that mission.

Why is hunting suddenly in vogue? I think the industry's reactionary mentality continues to hinder enterprise security while adversaries enjoy a free-for-all, easily circumventing traditional defensive stacks and exfiltrating record-breaking amounts of data. We can no longer wait until the CISO gets a call from law enforcement saying there's a problem.

Hunting can help shift the balance in the defender's favor, but it requires changing from a reactionary posture to an attacker's mindset. You can't stop a breach if you don't know exactly which attacker techniques must be blocked. Most adversaries – regardless of their objectives – must be able to gain initial access, escalate privileges, steal credentials, move within and across assets, evade defenses, and persist in networks. Detecting these functions is a key component of hunting because it tells you where to hunt. Instead of focusing retrospectively as each malware variant is discovered or indicators of compromise are revealed, organizations can hunt for and prevent whole classes of techniques, thus defending against unknown threats. Further, systematic hunting allows an organization to easily collect and analyze the right data across assets to find suspicious or malicious activity.

Hunting is often confused with "hacking back." However, retaliation must be left to the government and law enforcement, because attack attribution is surprisingly hard and revenge against adversaries with strong retaliation capabilities is a losing strategy. Instead, we can make life harder for adversaries by continuously hunting to detect, block, and evict them – to the point where it is no longer time and resource efficient for them to attack us.

Our goal in this book is to dispel misperceptions about the hunt mission and provide recommendations for structuring hunt teams and practical insights on employing cutting-edge hunt techniques. By adopting an offense-based strategy, enterprises can regain control of their networks and protect their most critical assets.

Jamie Butler
Chief Technology Officer
Endgame

Preface

No matter their industry sector, organizations around the world share a common challenge: finding an effective approach for rapidly identifying and acting on cyber threats. With an average "dwell time" of nearly 150 days before discovery, attackers have ample opportunity to plan and carry out the theft of intellectual property, customer data, and other valuable information – or to cause physical destruction. Moreover, with easy, inexpensive access to sophisticated hacking tools and "rent-a-hacker" services via the dark web, attackers have increased the variety and number of their attacks every year. To make it too hard for attackers to succeed, we need to leverage emerging technologies to harden our organizations and assets.

Existing attack detection tools look backwards in time. To discover what happened, they apply classic big data approaches such as discovery or search to collections of historical log data. Once a successful attack is discovered, they create rules to guide detection of the next occurrence of the same attack. The goal is to learn from the past to protect against future attempts. There's just one problem: the next attack will probably be different.

Fortunately, we're finding new ways to eliminate exposure to novel threats and vulnerabilities. These approaches rely upon blends of new technologies, including advanced data science, major advances in chip-level processing, and powerful cognitive visualization techniques. Two stand out.

The first is hunting, which seeks to turn the tables on attackers by establishing an active offensive motion against them within the virtual confines of the network footprint. Simply put, if you're only defending, you'll stay one step behind attackers and never take control. Hunting takes the fight to the front lines. It finds attackers before they do damage—not afterwards. Hunting makes it harder for attackers to succeed.

The second approach creates awareness of current activities based on behavior. Individual abnormal events and combinations of connected events are quickly highlighted for investigation. These include malicious, never-before-seen actions and movements hiding within the noise of normal events. Behavior-based solutions, such as Accenture's Cyber Intelligence Platform, maximize real-time awareness and harden defenses while taking advantage of current attack intelligence.

Hunting and behavior-based intelligence platforms address the need for state-of-the-art cybersecurity tools. Together, they enable organizations to rapidly "point and shoot" adversaries. For more information, or to arrange a demonstration of either approach, please visit https://www.endgame.com.

Vikram Desai
Managing Director, Global Lead Security Analytics
Accenture

Introduction

For many years, we (the security community) fought the good fight against the adversaries attacking our organizations' systems. We applied patches for our operating systems and applications as quickly as feasible. We configured and reconfigured software to comply with security checklists and benchmarks while still providing the necessary functionality. We relied on antivirus software, firewalls, intrusion prevention systems, and other tools to prevent attacks.

It's time to admit that the conventional approach to enterprise security is insufficient. We need to take a step back and reconsider our assumptions. Instead of focusing all our energy on reactive security and waiting for an alert, we should take a proactive approach to security, striving to find adversaries and purge them from our environments as quickly as possible.

This doesn't mean that we throw away existing security controls for prevention; prevention is still incredibly important. But it does mean being more proactive in order to detect adversaries and evict them from our networks. The best way to accomplish the shift from a reactive to proactive posture is to hunt, which is the focus of this book.

Anyone who has responsibilities for securing or monitoring the security of systems and networks, detecting attacks, or responding to compromises will benefit from this book.

Chapters at a Glance

Chapter 1, "The Power of Hunting," explains the basic concepts of hunting, the motivations for hunting, and the benefits of hunting.

Chapter 2, "The Hunt Process," looks at each of the major components of the hunt, including the technical details of what's involved in executing each component.

Chapter 3, "The Challenges of Hunting," discusses common roadblocks to successful hunting and explains in depth how these challenges can best be addressed, with a focus on automated hunt technologies.

Chapter 4, "Hunt Readiness," shows how to get your organization ready to adopt and use hunt practices that work in concert with hunt technologies.

Chapter 5, "The Hunt Experience," provides a case study based on a fictional enterprise and situation that depicts the hunt process from the hunter's perspective. This chapter takes a deep dive into the hands-on details of hunting.

Chapter 6, "Hunt Technology Selection," discusses the most important practical considerations to keep in mind when choosing an automated hunting solution.

Glossary provides useful definitions for key terminology (appearing in *italics*) used throughout this book.

Helpful Icons

Tips provide practical advice that you can apply in your own organization.

When you see this icon, take note as the related content contains key information that you won't want to forget.

Proceed with caution because if you don't it may prove costly to you and your organization.

Content associated with this icon is more technical in nature and is intended for IT practitioners.

Want to learn more? Follow the corresponding URL to discover additional content available on the Web.

Chapter 1

The Power of Hunting

- Review recent changes to threats that impact defenses and increase the need for hunting
- Understand the basics of hunting and the most important benefits it can provide

nformation technology (IT) security has never been as important as it is today. Our society's near-absolute dependency on IT, coupled with increasingly sophisticated adversaries, means that virtually all sensitive information, from personal medical and financial records to an organization's most prized intellectual property, is at risk.

A glance at today's headlines underscores the scope of this problem. Data breaches and other compromises happen all the time. The purpose of this book is to show you how to use hunting to reduce your own organization's chances of being compromised. *Hunting* is the process of proactively looking for signs of malicious activity within enterprise networks without prior knowledge of those signs, then ensuring that the malicious activity is removed from your systems and networks.

TIP

This chapter and Chapter 2 set the stage for the rest of the book by providing important background information on threats, defenses, and the basics of hunting. These chapters are meant to be shared with others who are unfamiliar with hunting to help educate them about the fundamentals and explain why hunting is rapidly becoming a critical component of modern security programs.

Advanced Threats

The threats against the data on our systems and networks are increasingly adept and sentient, making them much harder to stop. Let's look at threats in terms of the individuals and groups causing them, and the ways in which these individuals and groups attack organizations.

Adversaries

Today a wide range of adversaries pose threats to organizations. Some are highly skilled and primarily rely on tools and techniques they develop, while others rely mostly or entirely on tools developed and distributed elsewhere. Some adversaries are lone actors, but others are teams and groups such as nation states, criminal organizations, and hacktivist groups.

CAUTION

While most adversaries are external, many breaches are performed by organizational insiders. This book focuses on hunting for external adversaries, but don't forget about internal adversaries and the threats they pose to their own organizations. Some insiders are obviously difficult to detect, such as a colleague who steals unattended printouts containing sensitive data. However, many insiders use some of the same tools and techniques that external adversaries use, which means that hunting can play an important role in detecting malicious insider behavior.

What sets today's adversaries apart from previous generations is the sophistication of techniques. Adversaries are increasingly employing never-before-seen tools and tactics, including custom and polymorphic malware that defeats existing security technologies. They are building evasion techniques into their exploits and malware to disable or circumvent traditional security tools and gain access to networks and the assets connected to them.

The kill chain

Adversaries rarely perform a single attack and gain immediate access to their ultimate target. Typically, adversaries execute attacks in stages to make their way through an enterprise, hopping from system to system, to eventually reach the sensitive data or services they are seeking. These stages, generally performed over an extended period, are collectively referred to as a *cyber kill chain*, or simply a *kill chain*.

The concept of the kill chain originated within military organizations to explain the structure of physical attacks. Lockheed Martin subsequently adapted this term to the electronic world to describe how advanced adversaries perform compromises, thus coining the term "cyber kill chain."

The kill chain has seven primary stages:

1. **Reconnaissance:** The adversary surveys the organization's environment, personnel, etc. to identify and characterize the targets.

2. **Weaponization:** The adversary develops or customizes malware and/or other malicious tools to be used against the organization.

3. **Delivery:** The adversary delivers the malicious payloads to selected assets.

4. **Exploitation:** The adversary uses the malicious payloads to take advantage of vulnerabilities or other weaknesses in the assets in order to gain access.

5. **Installation:** During or after gaining access to targets, the adversary establishes a presence on them to maintain that access, often at an administrator level. Adversaries accomplish this through the installation and execution of malicious code and tools, the escalation of privileges from guest or user level to a higher level, and the establishment of persistent methods of retaining access even if the original access method becomes unavailable in the future. Adversaries move laterally through the enterprise from target to target by maintaining their presence on past targets and performing exploitation to new targets.

6. **Command and Control (C&C):** At this point, the adversary has reached the ultimate target, exploited it, and installed code to maintain a presence. These actions enable the adversary to establish command and control (C&C) capabilities for the target.

7. **Action on Targets:** In the last stage of the kill chain, the adversary uses the C&C capabilities to achieve the desired objectives, such as exfiltrating sensitive data from the target to an external location, or manipulating the integrity of data stored on the target to benefit the adversary.

Weakening Defenses

As adversaries have become highly motivated by financial, political, and ideological aims to pursue data breaches and other compromises, they've realized the importance of avoiding defenses. By using a stealthy attack approach that takes advantage of defensive weaknesses, adversaries can maintain their presence within an organization for weeks, months, or even years.

One of the main reasons that organizations' defenses have weakened so much is the erosion of the traditional perimeter. Organizations rely on firewalls, intrusion prevention systems, and other network security controls at the perimeter to prevent threats from entering their internal networks. Today, with laptops and mobile devices operating and connecting from outside the perimeter, and many servers and services hosted in external clouds, the perimeter is porous, riddled with additional, highly dynamic entry points provided by both enterprise and personal devices.

As the perimeter dissolved, adversaries learned how to evade detection by security technologies that rely on signature-based methods. These technologies can't keep up with highly dynamic and customized exploits and malware. *Indicators of compromise* – distinct characteristics that correspond to a particular campaign or piece of malware – are often unique for each instance of an attack, making detection through known signatures unlikely or impossible.

DON'T FORGET

Although the focus of this book is hunting for external threats, insider threats are also a major concern. They often involve an employee's abuse of privileges granted by the organization, thus avoiding the need to use malware or other exploits. Most security tools can't differentiate an insider's malicious actions from benign actions. Many insiders simply copy data from their computers to a USB flash drive or other removable media, an action that may go completely unnoticed by security controls.

As the result of weaker defenses and stronger threats, preventing compromises is much harder and detecting them takes much longer. On average, adversaries are present within an organization for 146 days before they are detected, and it often takes weeks or months more to fully remove them. The period during which an adversary maintains a continuous presence within an organization, generally achieved through malicious processes running on one or more assets, is better known as *dwell time*. (The source of the dwell time statistic above is Mandiant's M-Trends 2016 report.)

Hunting Basics

The primary goal for hunting is to reduce dwell time. This helps the organization reduce the damage and loss it incurs from compromises. Hunting accomplishes these goals by bringing an offense-based approach to securing your organization's systems.

To understand what that means, let's first look at the current state of security. It relies almost completely on passive, reactive defenses. Once security professionals become aware of a compromise that's been detected through standard, passive security controls or reported by an external party, they react to that compromise and execute incident response procedures to recover.

Unfortunately, this leaves a great deal to be desired. When an organization relies on passive, reactive defenses, less-skilled adversaries may be stopped quickly, but more-sophisticated adversaries can easily evade the defenses and reside undetected within the organization's systems and networks.

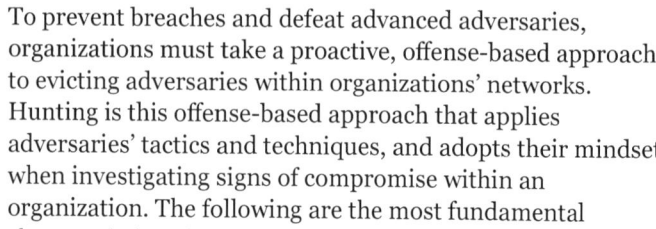

DON'T FORGET

To prevent breaches and defeat advanced adversaries, organizations must take a proactive, offense-based approach to evicting adversaries within organizations' networks. Hunting is this offense-based approach that applies adversaries' tactics and techniques, and adopts their mindset when investigating signs of compromise within an organization. The following are the most fundamental characteristics of hunting:

- ☑ Proactive – It seeks out adversaries without relying on alerts by finding traces left behind by even the most sophisticated adversaries.

- ☑ Stealthy – It looks for adversaries using methods that hide its presence from those adversaries.

- ☑ Methodical – It follows a logical and justifiable course when determining what adversaries are likely to do and where they are most likely to be found.

Each individual who hunts on behalf of an organization is simply known as a *hunter*. The hunter is responsible for looking for and identifying known and unknown adversaries within the organization's assets, then analyzing their actions and behavior to determine their intent and impact. Hunters are usually responsible for removing the adversaries from the organization, including eliminating their entry methods to prevent further damage. In some environments, hunters may also be in charge of conducting recovery efforts for assets affected by adversaries.

Hunting and the Security Program

It's important to think of hunting as a part of the overall security program. Although hunting may be somewhat separate from other security activities, it has critical dependencies with those activities.

In terms of input, hunting needs to be prioritized based on what parts of the organization adversaries are most likely to have already compromised or to attempt to compromise. This information may come from a variety of sources, ranging from intrusion prevention system alerts and threat intelligence data to enterprise risk assessments and business impact analysis reports.

In terms of output, the findings from hunting have repercussions for security throughout the organization. Hunting not only identifies low-level vulnerabilities and other weaknesses being exploited by adversaries, but it can also identify high-level security design and architecture issues that may only be addressable through long-term initiatives. Hunting can also find new trends in threats that may require the organization to shift security resources, such as investing in new security controls or retraining staff.

The Benefits of Hunting

The main goals of hunting are to:

1. Reduce dwell time by expediting adversary detection and reducing investigation and forensic costs.
2. Evict adversaries with minimal business disruption.

Hunting enables an organization to identify, characterize, analyze, and remove advanced adversaries as early in the kill chain as possible, which can be facilitated with automated technologies that support the hunt. Stopping adversaries early in the kill chain generally hinders them from reaching their ultimate target.

TECH TALK

At a more technical level, there are additional benefits to hunting. Hunting can find attacks that can't readily be detected by passive defenses. For example, hunting is effective at finding previously unknown attacks because it doesn't depend on already knowing the signs of a specific attack. Similarly, hunting can find attacks that don't use malware because it isn't specifically focused on malware-based attacks. Many passive defenses rely on prior knowledge of malware characteristics (i.e., signatures) and can't identify attacks that don't use malware.

The Endgame Philosophy

Endgame's philosophy is that organizations must think like adversaries to eradicate their known and never-before-seen adversaries from their enterprise networks. At its core, this philosophy necessitates a shift from reactive to proactive security. Instead of waiting for a compromise to be found after the damage has been done, hunters actively search for signs of compromise, greatly accelerating detection of and responses to attacks.

Endgame's philosophy has three other important components:

- Hunting must be done with stealth in mind. Just as adversaries rely on a variety of stealth techniques to stay undetected, hunters must adopt similar techniques so the adversaries can't detect them.

- Hunting must instantly detect and stop adversaries at all stages of the kill chain from gaining unauthorized access to critical systems to stop the damage they can inflict on the organization.

- Hunting technologies enable hunters to surgically respond to advanced threats without disrupting business processes.

Endgame's technology provides extensive automation, empowering less-experienced staff to hunt effectively. This technology is based on the experience of Endgame's staff, who have developed hunting methods and technologies for the intelligence and defense communities and adapted them for mainstream enterprise networks.

Endgame experts include highly experienced hunters, malware researchers and analysts, security operations experts, hackers, and data scientists. Many of these experts are from the intelligence and defense communities, so they remain current with cutting-edge advances in hunting methods and technologies, adversary attack techniques, and other aspects of the hunt.

In summary: Thinking offense, just like the adversary, leads to smarter hunting.

Chapter 2

The Hunt Process

- Learn the basic phases of the hunt cycle
- Do a deep dive into each hunt cycle phase to understand how it involves people, processes, and technology

The process of hunting involves a series of phases better known as the *hunt cycle*. This chapter provides an overview of the overall hunt cycle, then takes a detailed look at each of the hunt cycle phases.

Hunt Cycle Overview

Endgame's hunt cycle has four phases, as depicted in Figure 2-1:

1. Survey – discover assets in the environment, determine which assets an adversary is most likely to target, and deploy sensors to assets to monitor them and collect data on any malicious activity.

2. Secure – lock down the monitored assets to ensure threats already in the environment are prevented from moving laterally and gaining further access. The secure phase also prevents execution of new malware and other exploits.

3. Detect – use the hunt sensors' automated detection and data collection capabilities to find evidence of successful and failed attacks, and identify adversaries by analyzing the collected data.

4. Respond – stop the attack by disrupting the adversary's access and preventing it from being regained, repair damage to compromised assets, and inform the appropriate personnel of the actions taken by the hunters and the weaknesses that still need to be addressed.

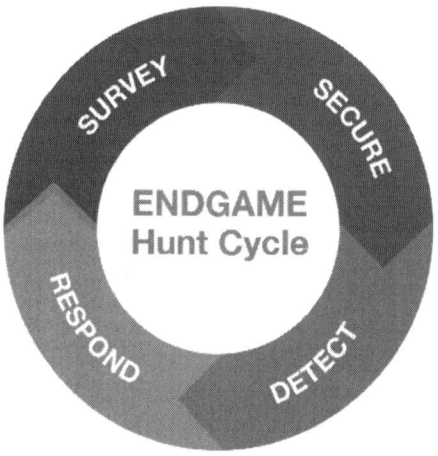

Figure 2-1: The Endgame hunt cycle

Some phases of the hunt cycle naturally receive greater emphasis than others. For example, the Survey phase – selecting the assets to hunt on and determining what data to collect – is likely to take far less time than the Detect and Respond phases. However, there's no magic formula for how much attention each phase should receive.

Hunt teams need to be mindful of two important items throughout the hunt cycle: risk assessment and communication. In terms of risk assessment, hunters always need to maintain situational awareness of the organization's security posture and be prepared to alter their hunting actions or plans as needed based on new information, emerging threats, and other changes to the organization's risk. Hunters also rely on risk assessment principles to guide their decision making during the hunt, such as deciding when to stop monitoring an adversary, and acting to remove that adversary from the asset.

Communication is just as important as risk assessment, if not more so. Hunters must keep each other and all other affected personnel informed of their actions, their findings, and their mitigations for breaches and other compromises. Without providing prompt and clear communication on significant matters, hunters may inadvertently disrupt the organization's operations, delay the deployment of additional resources to help during critical situations, and otherwise make the hunt considerably less effective than it could be.

Now that we've taken a high-level look at the hunt cycle, let's examine each phase in more detail.

Survey Phase

The first phase of the hunt cycle is to survey the environment. The purpose of this survey is to determine on which assets in the environment hunting will take place. In addition, the hunter must implement the necessary monitoring capabilities on each of the selected assets and begin collecting data from them. Let's look at these components in detail.

Select assets

Selecting the assets to hunt on next may sound simple, but it's incredibly important. If a critical asset is overlooked or mischaracterized, the hunters may not look for threats on that asset in a timely manner, if at all. As a result, the dwell time for any adversaries on the asset may be extremely long, and additional loss of sensitive information may occur.

In an ideal world, hunters would identify every asset within the organization through network-based scans or other means and hunt on all of them. Alternatively, hunters could perform the hunt on every asset that stores or processes sensitive information, plus every asset that provides access to those assets, and so on. Unfortunately, these approaches would end up involving just about every asset.

Few organizations, if any, have the resources to actively hunt on all their assets all the time, so it's vital that the assets perceived as the greatest risk to the organization are prioritized for hunting purposes.

Let's take a step back and think about the factors hunters should consider when deciding which assets to hunt on. Examples include the following:

☑ The current security posture of the asset. For example, vulnerability scans and other vulnerability assessment methods may indicate that an asset has extremely weak security. This means it's more likely to be compromised and may merit immediate attention from a hunter to prevent further damage.

☑ The direct value of the asset. An asset that contains highly sensitive data or performs mission-critical transactions should be prioritized over an asset with no access to sensitive data or applications, because the consequences of compromising the former are so much worse.

☑ The indirect value of the asset. Compromising a system administrator's laptop might allow an adversary to connect to many other assets within the organization using administrative privileges, so that laptop would be much more valuable than others.

☑ The resources, including manual effort and specialized tools, needed to perform hunting on the asset as compared to others.

TIP It's best if hunters think about these considerations based on both their inside knowledge of the assets and an external adversary's likely knowledge and assumptions about the organization's assets. For example, an adversary can reasonably guess that a retailer has databases containing personal information for its customers and personnel records for its current and former employees, so these obvious targets should be candidates for the hunt.

Just like adversaries, hunters must conduct research to uncover information about the assets, such as which operating systems and applications they use. Hunters must perform network reconnaissance to uncover information about the organization's critical assets, then take that intelligence into consideration when selecting assets for hunting.

Monitor assets

Once the hunters have selected the assets to hunt on, the next step is to ensure that the necessary monitoring and data collection capabilities for each of the assets are in place. The goal of monitoring the assets is visibility into the activities occurring within them, as well as between an asset and any others, in order to observe actions performed by adversaries and maintain situational awareness for current threats.

Achieving full visibility into security events for the hunt generally requires both host and network monitoring. Network-level monitoring is usually present in the enterprise through intrusion prevention systems and other network-based security technologies. Hunters should have access to the logs from these technologies to help them verify the sources of suspicious activity and correlate activity across assets.

Host-level monitoring is best accomplished by installing hunt sensors on these assets. Chapter 3 contains much more on hunt sensors, but basically a *sensor* performs a wide range of hunt functions within an asset. An alternate approach to installing a hunt sensor is to use a sensorless monitoring method. There are limitations to a sensorless approach because it relies on user mode and operating system data retrieved through an application programming interface (API). A sensorless approach can't provide continuous monitoring, creating blind spots in the data. Another weakness is its dependence on data from system log files, which can be altered by the adversary, thus giving low confidence in the data collected from them.

TECH TALK For the purposes of the hunt, host-level monitoring usually focuses on certain types of activities, such as unexpected and anomalous features of the filesystem, as well as particular processes, network connections, and configuration settings (e.g., registry keys on Microsoft Windows assets). Such anomalies are often evidence of a current or past compromise. See Chapter 5, "The Hunt Experience," for deeper technical insights into this topic.

It's important that monitoring and data collection be implemented in such a way that adversaries can't disable or evade it. If given the opportunity, adversaries will shut off logging and clear existing logs, disable security controls that prevent and detect attacks, and inject their own malicious software at a low level within assets to avoid detection and removal.

DON'T FORGET

Host-level monitoring should be deployed stealthily and be at or below the level of the attacker to minimize adversaries detecting and tampering with hunt sensors. See the "Concealing the Hunt from Adversaries" portion of Chapter 3 for more details.

Secure Phase

Many people don't realize that prevention is a major component of hunting. The unspoken assumption is that securing assets—everything from applying patches and configuring software securely to installing, monitoring, and maintaining network and host-based enterprise security controls—is the responsibility of system administrators, security administrators, and other operational staff.

Unfortunately, this is a short-sighted approach based on a reactive, passive defense. While operations should certainly play the largest role in fundamental security activities for assets, hunters are perfectly positioned to take asset security a step further through the use of hunt sensors.

TECH TALK

Some hunt sensors provide mechanisms that can prevent the use of various exploit and attacker techniques. Examples of these techniques include:

- ☑ Injecting malicious code into a process
- ☑ Executing unauthorized code
- ☑ Misusing legitimate credentials
- ☑ Escalating privileges (often to gain administrator rights)
- ☑ Moving laterally from asset to asset

In addition to defending against these techniques, securing assets is important to the success of the hunt because it's securing the hunting ground itself. If the hunting ground is unsecured, it is strongly in the adversaries' favor, and they will be able to compromise assets more quickly and go undetected. In contrast, when the hunting ground is well secured, adversaries are forced into the open to the extent possible, and have to work much harder and progress more slowly to avoid detection.

Another important reason to strongly secure the hunting ground is protecting the hunters' asset monitoring capabilities from adversaries. In some cases, it may be better to secure the assets first and then implement monitoring on those assets.

Detect Phase

At this point in the hunt cycle, the hunter has selected assets for the hunt, established monitoring and protection capabilities for those assets through hunt sensors, and ensured that the hunt sensors are preventing any additional movement of the adversaries to limit further damage and loss.

Detect attacks

At the heart of the hunt is the ability to detect attacks as early as possible in the kill chain. Hunters must gather data that could uncover suspicious activities and analyze that data to find the adversaries hiding among all the noise. Indications of malicious activity can appear within a single set of data or can be found by looking for anomalies across many assets. Hunters can leverage analytic capabilities provided by their hunt platform, along with their own abilities to understand the meaning and significance of the collected data, to ultimately identify the compromises.

Finding anomalies in the collected data that indicate the presence of attackers is far more effective at detecting the most advanced threats than searching for known indicators of compromise, which change rapidly and often aren't useful by the time they make it into detection tools. If technologies to secure the hunting ground are in place, those capabilities can provide high-confidence detections of malicious activity.

DON'T FORGET

Remember that it's not hunting if the hunter already knows what to look for.

Perform analysis

The sheer volume of data captured by hunt sensors monitoring the assets can be overwhelming. Fortunately, hunt technologies also offer analysis capabilities. Here are some commonly offered capabilities:

- ☑ Finding in-memory techniques like process injection, process anomalies such as remote code execution, statistically unusual running processes, and anomalous persistence on monitored assets

- ☑ Comparing observed events to expected events to identify outliers and other suspicious activity that may be worthy of further investigation

- ☑ Correlating events or multiple views of a single event occurring within an asset that are all part of the same attack

- ☑ Determining the full extent of the breach and pivoting across the enterprise network to stop the same compromise on other assets

- ☑ Tracing an attack across networks and other assets, which may include correlating events among assets

TIP

Automating analysis is extremely helpful to the hunter, and in most cases it's absolutely essential to successful hunting. Automation enables tier 1 and tier 2 analysts to hunt and provides senior analysts the ability to scale their hunting to include more assets.

Malware Analysis and Data Science

Malware analysis is incredibly demanding in terms of the hunter's time and knowledge. Therefore, it's critical to automate it as much as possible to reduce the workload on hunters and to speed the analysis process so that malware can be identified and eradicated more quickly.

An interesting approach is to apply *data science* methodologies, which are quantitative and computational methods for analyzing structured and unstructured data. *Natural language processing (NLP)* — techniques for analyzing unstructured text and extracting meaning from human languages — is one data science approach that can be applied to malware analysis. Another approach is *machine learning*, which refers to computational techniques that identify patterns and learn by processing and analyzing data. A malware analysis tool that uses NLP and machine learning techniques can parse malware code into its constituent components, evaluate the meaning of each component, and understand how those components relate to each other.

This approach can be far more effective than traditional techniques that rely on matching long sequences of bytes or finding certain instructions in a particular order. NLP and machine learning-based malware analysis not only can parse previously unknown malware into its individual instructions, but also understand the context for each instruction and take that context into account when determining the intent of the malware.

For more information, see the Endgame white papers "Automate the Hunt for Malicious Binaries with Data Science Techniques" and "Hunting for Malware with Machine Learning" at https://www.endgame.com/resources.

Respond Phase

Once a hunter has found a compromised asset, the hunter may choose to monitor the adversary for some time to collect additional information on the adversary's techniques, intent, and goals. Ultimately, however, the hunter's objective will be to evict the adversary and stop any further damage or loss, and report findings from the hunt.

Remove the adversary

An adversary's presence on an asset depends on three things:

1. Code execution. Adversaries must be able to execute malicious code or misuse existing tools such as Windows PowerShell already on the assets. Otherwise, they can't control the asset, harvest its data, etc.

2. Communications. The adversary maintains a presence by relying on automated command and control (C&C) communications between the asset and a remote system the adversary controls. These communications are sometimes tunneled or proxied through other compromised systems on the network.

3. Persistence. *Persistence* is the ability to maintain access to a compromised asset even if the original entry points have been remediated and are no longer usable by the adversary. There are many methods for establishing persistence, from using stolen user credentials to relying on a backdoor installed by the adversary onto the asset.

Remediation may be the hunter's responsibility or deemed outside the scope of the hunter's duties and handed off to an incident response team. Regardless, all traces of the adversary must be removed in a coordinated fashion for remediation to be successful. Malware should be removed, misuse of compromised legitimate credentials mitigated, and persistence removed.

Chapter 5, "The Hunt Experience," provides a detailed case study that includes more information on the adversary removal process.

Although a compromise may involve only one asset, adversaries usually compromise multiple assets to reach the ultimate target asset. Removing an adversary from the organization often requires expanding the hunt to include other assets where the adversary may have a presence, thus identifying the full extent of the breach and enabling the creation of a comprehensive and coordinated response plan.

Once ready to stop an attack and remove the adversary, the hunter must decide how the organization can accomplish those objectives while minimizing disruption to operations. Sometimes it's necessary to block access to a compromised asset or take that asset offline to prevent further damage. In other cases a narrower, more precise remediation approach, like suspending the thread, effectively evicts the adversary without any business disruption.

Hunters must also consider the scope of the attacks and compromises. For example, an adversary may be affecting many assets, in which case the hunter may need to act quickly to stop the attack on all those assets. It's important for hunters to have automated tools to aid them in stopping attacks and removing adversaries. Chapter 3 provides more information on these tools.

Hunters usually have other responsibilities as well. For example, they need to ensure that any mechanisms implemented by an adversary to maintain persistent access for future use, such as installing backdoors onto an asset, are identified and removed to prevent the adversary from readily re-entering the organization.

Report findings

TIP Although reporting findings comes at the very end of the hunt cycle, hunters must document their actions throughout the course of the hunt. Trying to recall accurately all the significant actions, the sequence and timeline of events, and other details after the hunt is completed is often impossible. Partial documentation may also be needed during the hunt, such as briefing others within the organization on the status of a potential compromise being investigated by the hunter.

CAUTION Hunters must be careful to strike the right balance between hunt documentation and primary hunt goals. Spending an hour documenting hunt actions while an adversary exfiltrates sensitive data from the organization is not a wise use of time. Instead, hunters should strive to document enough information so they can fill in the blanks when time permits. Automated tools may also be helpful in keeping track of hunter actions.

In addition to documenting their account of the hunt, hunters must document their findings. Following are examples of key findings to report:

☑ The root cause or causes of the compromise (what weaknesses allowed the compromise to occur)

☑ A description of the techniques used by the adversary

☑ Indicators of compromise to be used for finding similar compromises on other assets

☑ Lessons learned and areas for improving future hunts

☑ Recommendations for short-term and long-term changes to the organization's security program and hunting processes

The Endgame Hunt Cycle

Based on many years of real-world hunting experience, Endgame's experts have pioneered the Endgame hunt cycle, which is depicted in Figure 2-1 at the beginning of this chapter. The Endgame hunt cycle establishes a hunting methodology that enables security analysts to stay ahead of adversaries by detecting them at all stages of the kill chain. Endgame automates the hunt cycle to stop adversaries before damage and loss occur.

The Endgame hunt cycle recognizes that the hunt won't succeed unless the assets are well secured. Without robust prevention in place, the hunter will face an endless series of compromises from a wide variety of adversaries instead of being able to focus on stopping advanced adversaries who could be hidden in the noise of compromises.

For more information on the Endgame hunt cycle, see the "Endgame Platform Datasheet" available at https://www.endgame.com/resources.

Chapter 3

The Challenges of Hunting

In this chapter

- Understand the most important challenges that your organization may face during hunting
- Learn how to address each of these challenges to make your organization's hunting more effective and efficient

Chapter 2 explained the basics of the hunt process, and hinted at some of the challenges of hunting. This chapter focuses on four particularly important challenges:

- ☑ Expediting the hunt
- ☑ Enabling advanced analysis
- ☑ Supplementing signature-based detection
- ☑ Concealing the hunt from adversaries

The focus of this chapter is to provide practical recommendations for addressing these challenges. Implementing these recommendations should significantly improve your organization's hunting, reducing damage and loss.

Note that Chapter 4 complements this chapter. Chapter 4 is dedicated to understanding and addressing challenges involved in preparing people and processes for the hunt. This chapter focuses on the technological aspects of the hunt.

Expediting the Hunt

In many organizations, hunting is largely a manual process, with hunters collecting data through numerous tools, then dumping that data into spreadsheets and manipulating the data to prepare it for time-consuming and error-prone manual analysis. This approach simply doesn't work against today's adversaries.

Hunters need automation capabilities that enable rapid detection and eviction of adversaries as early in the kill chain as possible to prevent further damage and loss. Automation enables hunters to make the most of their expertise by handling all hunt tasks that don't rely on human interpretation of the data and decision making.

The heart of a centralized hunt automation solution for an enterprise is a *hunt platform*. It automates several types of hunt tasks, including the following:

- ☑ Asset discovery and characterization: probing and discovering their networked services and the connections to these services. This information helps the hunter to prioritize assets and identify likely attack vectors.
- ☑ Data collection capabilities: continuously monitoring assets to gather data on process execution, network connections, configuration settings, filesystem changes, and other potential artifacts of compromises.
- ☑ Prevention capabilities: stopping exploit execution, credential theft, lateral movement, and other attack techniques to preclude an adversary from gaining further access.
- ☑ Adversary detection capabilities: using a variety of techniques, such as outlier analysis and machine learning. For example, a hunt platform may discover a process executing on only one asset. This process, launched by an unfamiliar file running, periodically communicates with an unknown remote system. By putting this information together, a hunt platform enables a hunter to quickly determine that an adversary is using malware to control the asset and exfiltrate sensitive data from it.

☑ Remediation capabilities: quickly and precisely evicting a detected adversary. A hunt platform can take numerous actions simultaneously or sequentially. For example, it could block a network connection, kill the process associated with that connection, and delete the file used to execute that process, all without disrupting operations.

A hunt platform provides sensor software to be installed onto the organization's assets. This *hunt sensor* software is designed to automate hunt actions within a single asset, from data collection and attack prevention to adversary detection and remediation. A hunt platform also uses one or more *hunt servers* for hunt sensor management and maintenance, data storage and analysis, and other purposes.

Enabling Automated Analysis

Hunters benefit greatly from automating much of analysis. Advanced analytics enable hunters to resolve ambiguities and apparent conflicts in the collected data and explore high-priority data more efficiently. Hunters can also take advantage of advanced analytics to fine-tune detection and refine remediation strategies.

For example, efficiently hunting for domain generation algorithm (DGA) malware – malware that generates numerous domain names for C&C purposes – requires automation that leverages data science methodologies. Given the sheer size and diversity of domains per day per malware family, static analysis is simply not feasible. An automated classifier quickly categorizes DGA malware and provides a confidence level to allow the hunter to act more quickly and efficiently. You can see an example of an Endgame DGA classifier at https://github.com/endgameinc/SANS_THIR16.

Similarly, automated analysis enables hunters to focus on higher-order patterns and signals that are often lost when focusing on specific signatures. For instance, the data science methodologies are equally useful for hunting for Domain Name System (DNS) response errors, features, or other characteristics that deviate from the norm. In this regard, automated analytics help surface useful insights for the hunter, who then prioritizes and focuses on the most important anomalies.

Supplementing Signature-Based Detection

Signatures have been used to automatically detect attacks for decades. Although signatures can stop attacks that have been seen before, the customized nature of current attacks means that signatures can't detect them.

Hunt platforms can use indicators of compromise and other forms of signatures to detect some adversaries, but they must also monitor attempts to use attack techniques within assets to detect more sophisticated adversaries. Although most instances of malware are unique, nearly all malware uses common attack techniques, such as process injection, credential dumping, token stealing, and lateral movement. Non-malware forms of attack rely on these techniques too.

A hunt platform can constantly look for and stop attempts to use attack techniques by monitoring a relatively small number of chokepoints within each asset's operating system. Executing most malicious actions requires adversaries to use one of these chokepoints. Another helpful characteristic of a hunt platform is that it can look for patterns across assets that indicate malicious activity.

Concealing the Hunt from Adversaries

Many adversaries build evasion techniques into their exploits and malware to work around or disable traditional security tools. An identified security tool quickly becomes a circumvented security tool. Being detected by the adversary means game over. Adversaries can enable automated checks for running processes and services and can use a simple command to stop services and disable traditional security products.

Knowing that the adversary is looking for security capabilities, hunters must hide their presence to provide uninterrupted protection, track and contain adversary behavior, analyze their techniques, and ultimately evict them from the environment.

CAUTION

Here are some tips for hiding from the adversary:

☑ Deploy hunt sensors stealthily. If an asset is already compromised, the adversary may be doing its own monitoring, making it much harder to deploy a sensor unnoticed. The hunter should make the sensor look innocuous by removing indications of its purpose, making the sensor software instance unique, and bundling its installation with other software.

☑ Perform monitoring in memory. It's much harder for adversaries to find and manipulate software resident in memory than in files stored on a local hard drive.

☑ Camouflage sensor-related communications. When a hunt sensor finds something noteworthy or is asked by the platform to send data for analysis, it must have a means of communicating that information to the hunt platform. It's generally recommended to encrypt and authenticate all communications.

☑ Reduce the volume of the sensor's network communications. If all raw data captured by sensors was transferred to the hunt platform, this could tip off adversaries to the presence of the hunt sensor. Ideally, the sensor performs its own analysis and correlation, then transfers just the most important data to the platform.

Adversaries may want to target the hunt platform itself. Compromising a hunt server could allow an adversary to take over the hunt platform. This would have catastrophic consequences because the adversary could access many critical assets, along with information about their vulnerabilities that could be useful for future compromises. The following are tips for protecting your organization's hunt platform:

☑ Configure each hunt server to provide only the minimal necessary functionality, then secure each server as tightly as possible to make it much more difficult for adversaries to gain unauthorized access.

☑ Require mutual authentication for all new inbound and outbound network connections involving hunt servers. This prevents adversaries from connecting to the servers from unauthorized locations and ensures that servers aren't tricked into communicating with rogue assets.

Encrypt all communications between hunt platform components to prevent eavesdropping by adversaries and possible manipulation of management communications involving the hunt servers, sensors, and other platform components.

Endgame Advantages

Endgame offers a comprehensive hunt platform that automates the hunt for never-before-seen adversaries before any damage and loss occurs. The Endgame hunt platform has numerous advantages over other hunt technologies. Let's highlight a few of these advantages.

- Endgame has extensive automation capabilities. The Endgame platform automates asset discovery, sensor deployment, adversary detection, question-driven investigation, and response actions to reduce investigation time and stop advanced adversaries. Automation across the hunt process improves productivity of tier 1 and tier 2 analysts while enabling tier 3 analysts to scale their hunting across the enterprise.

- The Endgame platform operates stealthily to evade adversary detection It hides its presence from adversaries in terms of deployment, execution, and communication. Endgame hunt sensors have a unique footprint on each asset, thus providing signature diversity. Also, the Endgame platform encrypts all hunt-related communications between its components.

- The Endgame platform rapidly detects activity across all stages of the kill chain to stop adversaries from gaining a foothold. The platform protects enterprises against both malware-based and malware-less attacks by focusing on detecting the attack techniques rather than only known indicators of compromise.

Endgame is focused on solving the hard problem of finding threats in innovative ways, instead of reinventing the wheel and creating yet another solution that relies on observing filesystem changes. Endgame's approach enables instant detection and characterization of new threats, which in turn enables immediate and precise responses to those threats. These responses evict adversaries from the enterprise while minimizing or completely avoiding any business disruption.

For more information on Endgame's advantages, check out the archive of hunt webinars available at https://www.endgame.com/resources.

Chapter 4

Hunt Readiness

- Know what to keep in mind when defining hunting roles and responsibilities
- Learn what's involved in scoping the hunt, including developing the cyber risk assessment report, hunt policy, and rules of engagement documents
- Understand how to build and maintain hunters' capabilities

Chapter 3, "The Challenges of Hunting," focused on technologies for automating and otherwise supporting all phases of the hunt. People and processes are just as important for the success of the hunt as technologies, so this chapter complements Chapter 3 by covering the major non-technological components of hunting.

Defining Hunting Roles and Responsibilities

Defining the roles and responsibilities related to hunting is an important part of hunt preparation. Although the hunter is certainly first and foremost in terms of hunting, many other individuals and teams must be involved as well, and hunting can't succeed without their participation and involvement.

Common roles and responsibilities

Let's look at the most common roles and responsibilities related to hunting. Note that many other individuals and groups may be involved to periodically review the policy and rules of engagement to ensure that they're consistent with all organization policies, regulations, etc.

Every organization should have its own structure and job definitions related to security in general and hunting in particular. Each organization is unique in terms of its culture, security requirements, and risk appetite and profiles. This section illustrates the range of hunting responsibilities and suggests one way of distributing them.

IT operations personnel

IT operations personnel are usually responsible for daily deployment, monitoring, and maintenance tasks for the organization's IT assets and networks. This work, which includes security-related tasks such as installing patches and checking configuration settings, is primarily performed by IT staff who don't specialize in security. However, it may also involve the organization's Security Operations Center (SOC) team—for example, a security analyst who receives an off-hours notification of a new exploitable vulnerability that needs to be patched immediately.

In terms of the hunt, the designated operations and/or SOC personnel play a key role in ensuring that the IT assets are well secured under both typical and emergency conditions. They may also be called upon to help restore normal operations after an asset compromise.

Incident response team

As the name implies, usually the incident response team is responsible for responding to and recovering from compromises. The details naturally vary from organization to organization, but at their core, incident response personnel can be divided into two groups.

The first group, including lower-tier incident responders, has the primary responsibility for all incident response activities caused by basic malware and other less-advanced threats. This includes detecting these threats by monitoring the output of enterprise attack detection tools, eradicating the threats from the organization, and recovering from any damage they've caused.

When hunters find these threats while hunting for advanced threats, they often hand off response duties to this first group of incident response personnel.

The second group of incident response personnel encompasses the most senior incident responders and a variety of specialists, such as the following:

☑ Malware analysts, who use reverse engineering and other methods to learn the purpose of each unique instance of malware and determine its impact within the organization. These personnel often analyze malware on behalf of hunters to free hunters' time for other tasks.

☑ Forensic analysts, who use a wide variety of tools and techniques to collect and preserve evidence from assets and networks on behalf of hunters. Forensic analysts may also conduct specialized analysis of evidence to further expedite the hunt.

All incident response personnel would generally benefit from expanding their focus from just incident recovery to also include activities that occur early in the kill chain. This helps personnel find malicious activity before it progresses and potentially causes serious damage. It also better prepares incident response teams to identify the root cause of an incident.

CAUTION Although there are commonalities between hunting and incident response, hunters usually aren't part of the incident response team. The purpose of hunting is to proactively identify and eradicate advanced adversaries, while the purpose of incident response is far broader. See the "Hunters and the hunt team" section below for more information on hunters.

Security team

The incident response personnel and the hunters are usually part of a larger security team. This team has many responsibilities, including identifying, documenting, and reporting shortcomings in the organization's security plans, policies, procedures, and technologies, and recommending ways to address them. The goal is to make compromises more difficult for all adversaries while avoiding negative impact to the organization's legitimate users.

TIP The individuals who manage the security team usually have the ultimate responsibility for hunting. Duties include everything from reviewing and approving hunting plans, policies, and budgets to ensuring that the hunters are well trained and their priorities and goals are clearly defined. Without the support of security team management, hunting is unlikely to significantly improve organizational security.

Hunters and the hunt team

Chapter 1 introduced the concept of the hunter and outlined the hunter's primary responsibilities. Ideally, hunting is performed continuously so adversaries can be detected and stopped as quickly as possible. The reality is that some organizations don't have enough resources to support continuous hunting on all their key assets.

Organizations must carefully prioritize their hunting resources, which includes deciding whether hunters are dedicated to hunting or whether hunting is one of multiple responsibilities for particular security team members.

Smaller organizations are likely to have hunters with other responsibilities. These hunters may take turns hunting on a designated set of assets. They are also more likely to be responsible for actions after compromise discovery instead of handing off that work to other security team members.

Larger organizations typically have dedicated, full-time hunters, and those with robust hunting capabilities often have a dedicated hunt team. The hunt team usually includes a team lead and several hunters. Larger teams may also contain hunt analysts, such as malware and forensic analysts dedicated to supporting the hunt. In such a structure, the hunters focus on quickly identifying the presence of advanced adversaries and compromises, as well as prioritizing their handling, leaving other personnel responsible for evicting adversaries, remediating vulnerabilities, and recovering assets to their normal operating states.

Scoping the Hunt

Organizations planning to adopt hunting or already hunting in an informal, ad hoc manner should strongly consider formalizing their activities into a program that scopes all aspects of the hunt.

Without a formal hunt program, hunters and supporting personnel are much more likely to take actions that aren't in the best interests of the organization and could cause serious disruptions and damage.

TIP It's not generally necessary to put an enormous amount of effort into scoping the hunt. Many organizations choose to incorporate hunt considerations in their existing incident response program. Instead of writing completely new plans, policies, and procedures, the organization can amend existing incident response documents to include the hunt. This approach takes advantage of the areas of overlap between hunting and incident response, and also minimizes duplication of documentation between the two domains. However, for simplicity, this chapter assumes that that the organization has separate hunt plans, policies, and procedures.

The first step in scoping the hunt is reviewing and using the cyber risk assessment report, which documents the organization's hunting priorities. Next is the creation of a hunt policy, which establishes the organization's hunting requirements (and, in some cases, recommendations as well.) The policy, in turn, is the basis for defining the formal rules of engagement to be used by hunters.

The following sections address the use of cyber risk assessment reports and the creation of hunt policies and rules of engagement documents in more detail. Note that the organization should review all such documents at least once a year and make whatever updates are deemed necessary. More-frequent reviews and updates may be needed if there are significant changes to the organization's security requirements, attractiveness to adversaries, and other factors that may substantially increase risk.

Cyber risk assessment report

The cyber risk assessment report is a foundational document for all hunting efforts. It lists the organization's critical IT functions, grouping them by their relative priorities. For example, it may be vital to an organization's mission to have certain applications available at all times, while other applications can tolerate occasional outages. Another example is that an organization may be required by law to protect the confidentiality of certain customer information, otherwise severe penalties and damage to the organization's reputation will result.

The cyber risk assessment report also provides a threat assessment for the organization as a whole and for specific critical IT functions as appropriate. The threat assessment analyzes known threats, ranging from criminals and hacktivists to nation states and insiders.

The hunters usually aren't responsible for creating or maintaining the cyber risk assessment report. That's handled by the management team familiar with the organization's priorities and the critical IT functions. Hunters simply use the report as a source of information and prioritization guidance.

Policy development

The hunt policy contains all the requirements for hunting within the organization, without specifying step-by-step procedures or other low-level information. It's also common for the hunt policy to contain guidelines and recommendations. These often give hunters flexibility in deciding what to do or not do, while still encouraging certain actions and behaviors.

The contents of the hunt policy will vary from organization to organization, but at a minimum the following should be addressed:

Definitions

- ☑ How the organization defines key terms, including "hunt" and "hunt cycle"
- ☑ How hunting differs from vulnerability assessments, red teams, penetration testing, incident response, and other activities

External Requirements

- ☑ Which external laws, regulations, and other requirements place restrictions on hunting, and what those restrictions are

Personnel

☑ Whom the policy applies to, including employees, contractors, vendors, and others acting on behalf of the organization

☑ If there's a hunt team, what its structure will be and where within the organization's structure it will be located

☑ What the hunt roles will be and which responsibilities will be assigned to each role, including management roles

Hunt Technology Requirements

☑ Where hunt sensor software and other hunt components may or may not be deployed

☑ How hunt sensors must be configured, especially which aspects of IT assets they may or may not monitor, which types of potentially maliciously used techniques they must block, and what data they must provide to the centralized hunt platform

☑ How hunt sensors and other hunt components must be secured

☑ How hunt sensors and other hunt components must implement stealth principles

☑ Under which circumstances the hunt technology may initiate corrective actions automatically, and how these actions must take the organization's change management practices into account

☑ What the minimum requirements are for hunt-related logging, log security, and log management

☑ Which other security technologies, such as the SIEM, are to be recipients of hunt data

Metrics

☑ Which hunt performance metrics must be tracked

The organization should also have metrics for measuring the success of the hunt program. These aren't to be confused with hunt performance metrics, such as the average dwell time per compromise and per adversary. Rather, these are metrics that quantify the impact of hunting on the entire organization, such as the annual reduction in damage or improvement in IT availability. At first, hunt plan metrics may be highly subjective and thus have limited usefulness, but over time the hunt program should mature and the metrics can mature correspondingly.

Rules of engagement development

The *rules of engagement* specify requirements for hunters' actions during all phases of the hunt cycle, as well as activities such as communications and reporting that are relevant across phases. Requirements typically included in the rules of engagement specify:

- ☑ Under what circumstances the hunter must ensure that evidence of a compromise is gathered in a forensically correct manner

- ☑ Which corrective actions a hunter may perform without and with management approval, and how these actions must take the organization's change management practices into account

- ☑ When a hunter must escalate an issue to management and who must be notified of this escalation

- ☑ How a hunter must act when hunt actions inadvertently disclose sensitive information to the hunter and/or others

- ☑ How a hunter must act when hunt actions inadvertently disrupt operations

- ☑ How a hunter must act when a compromise has originated from a contractor, business partner, or vendor of the organization, or from an employee or other internal user

- ☑ What information the hunter may share with others, with whom it may be shared, and under what circumstances

- ☑ Whether or not the hunter may perform active reconnaissance, attacks, and/or other actions against an adversary

☑ What the hunter must document for each hunt, to whom the information must be communicated, and when this communication must occur

Hunters and Risk Assessment

Hunters must rely on risk assessment throughout the hunt to inform their decision making, including prioritization. Although some elements of risk assessment can be specified in policy requirements, most can't because every situation has unique characteristics. At best, an organization can document factors that hunters should consider when assessing or reassessing risk during the hunt, and perhaps provide some guidelines to express preferred strategies for risk assessment. A great place to specify these factors is the rules of engagement document.

Risk assessment guidance may be beneficial to hunters when making these types of decisions:

- Which asset should be the current focus of the hunt at any given time (see the "Survey" section of Chapter 2 for more on asset selection)

- How to allocate time to spend hunting on a particular asset (analyzing monitored security events, investigating possible compromises, characterizing adversaries, etc.)

- When to monitor an adversary's actions versus evicting the adversary and restoring normal operations as soon as possible

- When a hunter should stop investigating a compromise and hand off the remaining work to others

- When it's the right time to share information from a hunt with others

Building and Maintaining Hunters' Capabilities

Although all personnel with hunt-related responsibilities will periodically need training and other ways of building and maintaining necessary capabilities, hunters usually need to devote substantially more time and effort to improving their hunt performance. Many hunters are experienced security analysts, but all hunters need a broader range of skills for effective and efficient hunting. Let's look at several of these areas.

Security knowledge

Hunters obviously must have the ability to use hunt techniques and tools, including those typically used for red teaming and penetration testing. In addition, it's beneficial for hunters to have strong knowledge of enterprise security principles and how they are implemented through security architectures and technologies, as well as operational and management security controls. Hunters who understand how all the different areas of security interact and fit together will be more capable of finding adversaries and understanding what they're trying to do.

Other helpful areas of security knowledge for hunters include:

- ☑ Incident analysis and response techniques

- ☑ Techniques commonly used by adversaries

- ☑ Tools for detecting and analyzing attacks, malware, and other exploits, to include reverse engineering of malware as well as host and network forensics

TIP Hunters often find that automated hunt technology empowers security teams and reduces dwell time. With a robust hunt solution, even novice hunters may be quite effective because the technology brings all the necessary information together and helps the hunter understand its meaning and choose the best response.

IT knowledge

Hunters should have a solid understanding of the organization's IT assets and networks. Much of this knowledge is a prerequisite to grasping security. For example, a hunter should be familiar with the organization's enterprise architectures, especially applications, to understand how parts of an application (user interface, middleware, database server, etc.) are divided among assets and interact with each other.

Another example of important IT knowledge is familiarity with the internals – the inner workings – of the operating systems used by the organization's assets. Such knowledge is essential for investigating events and understanding their effect on each asset. Hunters should also be familiar with how operating systems and applications on the organization's assets are configured and maintained.

Hunting mindset

What distinguishes hunting from so many other aspects of defense is the requirement to think like an adversary. At a high level, this means that the hunter approaches the asset as an adversary would, focusing the hunt on the aspects of the asset that adversaries would focus on as well.

Decision-making

Decision-making is a vital skill for hunters. At key points in the hunt, hunters must assess the current state of security. Relying on their strong critical thinking skills, they must consider many factors before deciding what to do next and when to do it. Examples of decision-making points are presented earlier in this chapter within the "Hunters and Risk Assessment" sidebar.

Communications skills

Another important skill for hunters is the ability to communicate effectively with others. Communication may involve a wide range of audiences, from other hunters, security professionals, and system administrators to upper management, the legal team, and human resources personnel.

Endgame Training Resources

Endgame's comprehensive hunt platform solution is designed to be intuitive and easy to use. With minimal training on the solution, any tier 1 security analyst or operator should be ready to hunt effectively within the organization's networks. To help with this, Endgame has developed training resources to assist future hunters in understanding the following:

- Basic hunt concepts, such as the purpose of hunting, the hunt cycle, hunter roles and responsibilities, and the value of automation

- The mechanics of hunting, from conducting surveys of the enterprise to identify assets and then selecting assets for hunting, to detecting threats by observing and analyzing several parts of an asset's operating environment

- Detailed instruction in handling a compromise, including how to analyze its characteristics, assess the risk posed by the compromise and the associated adversary, and evict the adversary and resume normal operations as soon as possible

In addition, hunters may benefit from many other sources of information on attack techniques and exploits. Two examples of outstanding field guides for hunters are the *Red Team Field Manual (RTFM)* by Ben Clark and the *Blue Team Handbook: Incident Response Edition* by Don Murdoch.

Chapter 5

The Hunt Experience

- Learn technical hunt concepts by walking through a detailed case study that gives you a taste of the actual hunt experience
- Gain a better understanding of techniques for adversary detection, analysis, and eviction

The previous chapters explained high-level hunt concepts, processes, and planning to provide the overarching themes for the hunt. Now it's time to illustrate the hands-on aspects of the hunt: detecting adversaries, analyzing their behavior, and evicting them from the enterprise.

CAUTION This chapter presents a technical case study based on a fictional enterprise, situation, and hunter. The case study isn't comprehensive; it doesn't include every single automated activity, manual action, analytic challenge, or decision. For example, it doesn't mention every time the hunter should document something during the course of the hunt. It's not that these actions are unimportant, but rather that this is an illustrative example to depict certain aspects of the hunt.

The case study focuses on adversary detection, analysis, and eviction. It's not a how-to guide, with step-by-step instructions, because that would only be useful in a tiny percentage of actual hunts. Instead, it shows you technical considerations that occur throughout the hunt, including cases where the hunter must make crucial decisions regarding the security of the organization.

The Hunt Scenario

Meet Pat, who was just hired by a large electric utility company to be the hunt team lead on its brand new hunt team. Pat is an experienced hunter, but the other three members of the hunt team are new to hunting. These hunters have backgrounds in IT and tier 1 incident response, so they have a working knowledge of security.

To help bring the less experienced hunt team members up to speed on hunting, they are taking turns shadowing Pat to see hunting in action and learn about hunt techniques and tools firsthand. Today it's your turn to shadow Pat at work.

The organization's enterprise security suite hasn't recently identified any malicious behavior on the organization's internal networks. Without any particular events to investigate further, Pat decides to proactively hunt on the networks. Pat uses the organization's most recent cyber risk assessment report to determine priorities and select the assets to hunt on first.

Aspects of Pat's hunting covered in this chapter are:

- ☑ Preparation
- ☑ Investigation
- ☑ Adversary Removal
- ☑ Synopsis of the Hunt
- ☑ Hunt Reporting

Preparation

Pat needs to perform some preparatory tasks before hunting. These include determining hunt priorities, reviewing available information on the organization's IT assets and networks, understanding what's considered normal activity on the organization's assets and networks, and configuring and deploying the hunt sensor software on the assets selected for hunting.

CAUTION Most of these tasks aren't meant to be performed each time the hunter is getting ready to hunt. They're general preparatory activities that will make future hunts go more smoothly and be more effective. For example, the hunter can act immediately when a likely compromise is discovered. Another example is that the hunter can quickly reprioritize hunt activities as needed while gathering more information about a potential compromise.

Determine hunt priorities

Before proactive hunting starts, Pat needs to decide which assets should be the initial focus of the hunt. Pat needs guidance from the organization's management on the relative importance of various assets. In this company, the business intelligence division is responsible for creating the cyber risk assessment report. Once the report is ready, management reviews it and endorses it, then provides it to Pat and the rest of the hunt team.

Pat reviews the highest-priority group of IT functions in the report and translates those functions, which are described from a business perspective (e.g., "credit card processing systems"), into the corresponding IT asset information that the hunt team needs: IP addresses, hostnames, process names, usernames, etc.

The result of Pat's translation is the identification of 25 servers, workstations, and other IT assets that directly support the functions in the cyber risk assessment's highest-priority group. These assets will be the initial focus of the hunt.

Review available IT asset and network information

TIP

Pat asks for the company's latest IT network maps and asset inventory information. The network maps are a helpful starting point for identifying the assets on the networks, but keeping track of all assets currently on the network through maps usually isn't practical because of the highly dynamic and mobile nature of IT assets.

Pat will need to confirm as needed which assets of interest are currently connected to the network and to get more information on these assets, such as knowing which major applications each asset is authorized to run. The company maintains an asset inventory through automated means, so it's generally accurate in terms of knowing which assets have used the organization's networks in the past and what software they should be running. Pat uses the asset inventory to get additional information on the assets to be hunted on.

Understand what's considered normal activity

Pat knows that every asset is different in terms of what's considered normal activity. Each network is unique as well in terms of usage patterns, such as which assets communicate with each other, when this occurs, how they interact (e.g., network and application protocols), and how much information they pass back and forth.

A hunter who knows what's normal for an organization's assets and networks will be much better prepared to spot deviations from the norm. Pat is new to the company, so it's worth spending time talking with system administrators, incident responders, and other IT staff members to learn more about normal activity. This can be as simple as knowing what the typical work days and hours are for people in different roles within the company (e.g., standard users, managers, developers, system administrators.) This can also be complex, including gathering detailed information on which assets people in each role may access, and which applications are whitelisted (allowed) or blacklisted (prohibited) on the company's assets.

Configure and deploy hunt sensor software

For operational reasons, the company is employing an on-demand deployment strategy for hunt sensor software, as described below. Pat is responsible for ensuring that the hunt sensor software is deployed to all the assets included in the initial round of hunting.

TECH TALK

Before doing that, Pat must configure the default settings for the hunt sensors. The configuration determines which aspects of each asset the hunt sensors automatically monitor. Pat selects default settings that record important details of the operating system files and configuration settings, network connections, running processes, and logged in user accounts. All of this information may be crucial to Pat when hunting on these assets.

Hunt Sensor Deployment Strategies

Hunt teams can choose between two deployment strategies for hunt sensors:

- Enterprise-wide deployment. The hunter deploys hunt sensor software to all assets on the organization's networks to continuously monitor security events, collect data on those events, and alert hunters of suspicious behavior that may merit further investigation. This is useful for maintaining constant situational awareness and gaining insights into potential intrusions.

- On-demand deployment. The hunter deploys hunt sensor software to only those assets that need to have their security state investigated and only does so when that investigation is imminent. As soon as the investigation has been completed, the hunter removes the hunt sensor software from the assets. This is useful for highly targeted hunting driven by an organization's risk assessments and operational requirements.

The case study in this chapter illustrates on-demand deployment.

Investigation

Pat has completed all the preparatory activities. It's time to investigate the 25 selected assets for the presence of adversaries. This investigation is documented in four parts: scoping the investigation, gathering and analyzing information, expanding the investigation, and reprioritizing the hunt.

Scoping the investigation

TECH TALK

Because there's no evidence of compromises or other malicious activity involving these assets, the first step in this investigation is to scope the work by selecting which aspects of each asset will be examined initially. Pat determines that the most important things to look for all involve the execution of processes and services. These characteristics fall into three groups:

Currently running processes and services

Pat needs to examine the full path of the executable for each currently running process and service, to include the executable's filename. Pat also needs additional information on each executable. Questions to be answered include:

1. Should this executable be running on this machine? Does its full path seem reasonable? For example, is the executable running from the appropriate system or application directory?

2. Which user ran the executable? Does this seem reasonable?

3. Was the executable run from the command line? If so, what were the command line arguments?

4. Does the code in the running process or service exist in a file stored on the asset's disk? If no, why doesn't such a file exist? (This is not typically benign behavior.)

5. If the code is in a stored file, does the file's hash match the vendor's hash for the file? Does this file exist on other assets, is it in the same location, and does it have the same hash as the copies on the other assets?

6. Which network connections are bound to the process or service? For each connection, the IP addresses and ports used by both endpoints must be noted.

7. Does it appear that all the loaded modules (executables and DLLs) indicated by the Process Environment Block (PEB) and import tables for a particular process or service are appropriate?

8. Are all registry keys associated with the process or service in the correct locations?

9. Do all open file handles (the files that the process or service is reading from and/or writing to) make sense?

Recently run processes/services

Pat also needs to examine available information about processes and services that were recently executed. Such information is available from the Prefetch folder and the registry keys for Application Compatibility Cache (ShimCache). This information must be evaluated to see if the processes and services run on the asset make sense. For example, did the full path of the executable seem reasonable?

Processes/services set to run in the future

Finally, the processes and services set to run in the future must be examined to ensure that all the processes and services should be executed on the asset. The executables slated to be run can be identified in one of two places:

☑ Registry auto-run keys. The purpose of these keys is to list executables to be automatically run in the future, such as when the asset is rebooted or when a local user logs in.

☑ Scheduled tasks. Users can schedule a particular executable to run in the future and designate the date and time when it will be started.

Gathering and analyzing information

At this point, Pat has defined the scope of the investigation but hasn't yet collected the necessary information within that scope. Gathering this information from all 25 assets and analyzing it to identify any suspicious behavior is an arduous process. Fortunately, the company's hunt sensor software can automatically do this work on Pat's behalf, speeding up the hunt considerably.

DON'T FORGET

While the hunt sensor software is starting its work, Pat reminds you of three key concepts to keep in mind:

☑ Assume that the asset has already been compromised.

☑ Look for compromises at any phase of an attack, from an initial exploit to implants that the adversary is no longer utilizing.

☑ Consider how an adversary would think and react.

Pat uses the hunt platform to review the results from the hunt sensors, and Pat quickly discovers that the third server, which is the primary web server that the company's customers use, has a running process that seems suspicious.

TECH TALK

The IIS process (the Microsoft web server itself) has an unbacked executable. A DLL was loaded into the process's memory space but no file corresponding to that DLL exists on the server's disk. Normally, all code executing in memory comes from a file on disk with a filename ending in .exe, .dll. .sys, etc. Two common causes for an unbacked executable are

DLL injection and process hollowing attacks, where an adversary forces malicious code into a normal-looking process.

Pat also notices other suspicious process activity on the same web server. Specifically, notepad.exe was run from the command line by an account with administrator privileges. More importantly, the hunter recognizes the command line arguments to notepad.exe as PowerShell arguments. In other words, the notepad.exe file is really a renamed PowerShell.exe file. The adversary is running PowerShell on the web server and is trying to hide that by renaming the executable to something innocuous.

Expanding the investigation

Based on the process information for the web server, it appears that the web server has been compromised. Pat immediately focuses the hunt on that web server and expands the investigation to include any other company assets that have established connections to the web server. These assets might have been compromised by the adversary in order to reach the web server, or these assets might be the next targets of the adversary.

Pat initiates the installation of hunt sensor software on the additional assets and uses the sensors to gather and analyze the same types of information for these assets as was done for the hunt's original 25 assets.

TECH TALK

Pat also takes a closer look at the compromised web server. Additional information to be obtained includes the following:

- ☑ The usernames for all users currently logged into the server
- ☑ The open file handles for all suspicious processes and services executing on the server
- ☑ A copy of each file stored on disk that's related to the suspicious processes and services
- ☑ A memory dump for each suspicious process or service
- ☑ A packet capture of all network traffic for the server

Reprioritizing the hunt

While the hunt sensors are collecting and analyzing more information, Pat receives an alert from the hunt sensor on the company's most critical database server. This alert indicates the presence of an unknown persistent service on that server, so Pat immediately reprioritizes hunting to focus on the database server.

Pat bases this decision on the knowledge that a compromise of the database server is potentially much more damaging to the organization than a compromise of the web server because the database server holds the company's most important and valuable intellectual property.

DON'T FORGET

Throughout the hunt, hunters must constantly reprioritize their focus based on updated risk assessments, their understanding of the value of particular assets, and the security event information provided by hunt sensors and other enterprise security controls.

A quick review of the current and recent hunt sensor monitoring within the database server indicates that the server has an established, encrypted connection to an external IP address. Pat knows that such a connection is not typical for this server. Pat can also see that a large amount of data is being transmitted from the database server to the external IP address, and that the service associated with the network connection is the same service that generated the unknown persistent service alert.

Adversary Removal

All evidence points to an adversary exfiltrating sensitive data from the company via the compromised database server. Pat must act as quickly as possible to stop the compromise by disrupting the exfiltration communications. Possible methods for handling this situation include the following:

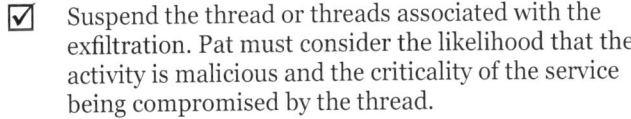

☑ Suspend the thread or threads associated with the exfiltration. Pat must consider the likelihood that the activity is malicious and the criticality of the service being compromised by the thread.

☑ Kill the service associated with the exfiltration. Pat would rather suspend the thread than kill the service because the latter can cause a significant disruption to operations. On the other hand, the entire service could be malicious, in which case suspending the thread won't be an effective form of remediation.

☑ Disable network access. Isolating the database server from other servers prevents further exfiltration and blocks the adversary from accessing the database server. Of course, this isolation also prevents all operational use of the database server, which will cause major production outages.

In this case, the hunt sensor indicates that there's a single malicious thread responsible for exfiltrating the data, and the service in question isn't malicious. This makes the decision easy. Pat orders the database server's hunt sensor to suspend the malicious thread. This action breaks the connection between the database server and the adversary while avoiding any disruption of the critical services that the database server provides to the company's customers, employees, vendors, business partners, and contractors.

Other Aspects of the Hunt

Pat has stopped the exfiltration from the database server and reduced the scope and impact of the breach. While this is a great start at handling this adversary, Pat knows there's much more work to be done.

There are 24 other assets from the initial scope of the hunt, plus dozens more assets that were added to the hunt when it was expanded because of the database server discovery. All of these assets need further investigation. It's likely that, in addition to the web server that Pat already identified, some of these other assets may also be compromised.

Each asset that's determined to be compromised needs to be handled by the incident response team at some point. Fundamental questions must be answered for each compromise by hunters, incident responders, and/or others with the necessary security expertise. Examples of such questions are:

- How did the adversary reach the asset?

- How did the adversary gain access to the asset after reaching it?

- What changes did the adversary make to the asset?

- Does the adversary still have access to the asset?

This information is necessary not only because it points out what recovery actions are needed, but also because it gives the hunters critically important information to aid in their investigations and in their reprioritization of hunt activities. For example, this information might indicate that other assets have been compromised, or it might highlight behavior patterns for the adversary that hunters can look for on other assets.

The rest of this chapter summarizes hunting related to the compromised database server only.

Synopsis of the Hunt

Let's fast forward to the end of the hunt investigation and recovery actions related to the compromised database server. Here's a synopsis of the most noteworthy actions:

1. Based on information provided by Pat and the database server's hunt sensor, Pat and other hunters searched all assets across the enterprise for the following:

    a. Any network connections involving the same external IP address that the database server was connected to and from which data was exfiltrated

      b. Any files with the same filenames and/or file hashes as the malicious files found on the database server

      c. Any registry keys matching the malicious registry keys found on the database server

2. The search for these characteristics identified an additional compromised asset: a Microsoft Exchange server. This server had the same malicious thread, executable file, and registry keys found on the database server, but the executable on the Exchange server was not currently running.

3. The company's incident response team forensically collected all files on the two servers associated with the malicious services, and they initiated chain of custody procedures. The files were turned over to the company's malware reverse engineers for further analysis.

4. Pat and other hunters removed all of the malicious files (including executables and other DLLs) and associated malicious registry keys from the compromised assets.

5. System administrators discovered that the compromised web server was missing a patch. Without this patch, the server was susceptible to users executing arbitrary code. The system administrators also determined that the web server and the database server had the same username and password for their local administrator accounts. This is how the adversary gained privileged access to the database server.

6. System administrators forced the change of all passwords for all local accounts on the web server and database server to prevent future reuse of any credentials that were compromised.

7. When Pat finished hunting on the database server, the hunt sensor was removed from the server in accordance with the company's on-demand deployment strategy.

Key Insights

Shadowing Pat has provided you with key insights into hunting, including the following:

- Hunt technologies enable hunters to detect advanced adversaries, including those already present within the enterprise who have bypassed other security controls.

- Hunters must constantly reprioritize their actions based on all available information.

- Hunters must think and react quickly in order to detect and evict adversaries while minimizing the impact to operations.

Hunt Reporting

Pat documented the findings and results for the hunt on an ongoing basis, issuing a separate report for each major compromise investigated through hunting. Pat's report for the database server compromise includes the following information:

- ☑ An executive summary that reiterates the most important points from the report

- ☑ The scope of the compromise, such as which business processes, IT assets, users, data sets, etc. were affected, in what ways they were affected, and how long they were affected

- ☑ The identity of the adversary, if known

- ☑ A timeline of the activities involving the compromise and the hunt investigation into that compromise

- ☑ A narrative corresponding to the timeline, indicating what the findings were at each step in the hunt process, which tools or techniques were used for each step, who received information from the hunters and when, what challenges or other issues were encountered and how they were resolved (or why they aren't yet resolved), etc.

- ☑ The root cause or causes of the compromise

Recommendations for improving the company's security and for making future hunts more effective, and the consequences to the company if these recommendations are not followed

Endgame's Support for the Hunt

Endgame's comprehensive hunt platform provides support for nearly every aspect of the hunt, including the following:

- Enabling proactive hunting to detect advanced adversaries who have bypassed other enterprise security measures

- Automating the hunt to scale your hunters' experience and analysis throughout the enterprise

- Protecting your assets by preventing the successful use of numerous exploit techniques

- Enabling hunters to evict adversaries by suspending threads, killing processes, deleting files, and performing other precise removal actions

- Performing in-depth analysis of all the gathered data using data science techniques, such as natural language processing and machine learning, to automate aspects of data collection, structuring, and correlation to identify the most significant events

- Concealing the hunt sensor and its operation from adversaries to prevent detection

- Supporting multiple deployment options for hunt sensor software: enterprise-wide and on-demand

Endgame provides a wealth of additional resources to further support hunters and the hunt. For example, Endgame experts presented their recommendations for hunting on a limited budget. Their slides demonstrating the use of many tools and techniques are posted at https://www.endgame.com/blog/hunting-cheap-part-1-architecture. Many other useful white papers, webinars, solution briefs, and data sheets are available from https://www.endgame.com/resources.

Chapter 6

Hunt Technology Selection

- Understand how a hunt solution's stealth, automation, work-flow support, and scalability strongly affect the hunter's ability to stop adversaries
- Increase your awareness of how a solution's enterprise integration characteristics can significantly change the breadth and depth of the positive impact of hunting on your organization

The previous chapters mention many desirable attributes for a hunt solution, specifically the hunt platform and the processes and procedures supporting use of that platform. This chapter concludes the book by reiterating the most important attributes of hunt solutions and providing new insights into these attributes.

Stealth

An adversary who discovers an organization's security controls can disable or tamper with them, or simply alter attack plans to avoid detection by those controls. These tactics illustrate why it's so important for the hunt solution to be stealthy, hiding its presence from adversaries. Organizations should look for hunt technologies that offer the following characteristics supporting stealth:

☑ Signature diversity: Today's malware looks for static fingerprints of hunt technologies, such as the existence of certain processes, files, and network ports on an asset. Stealthy hunt technologies must provide fingerprint control, allowing organizations to control how the hunt software looks to adversaries.

☑ Kernel-level presence: Hunt technologies must reside at or below the level of adversaries to stop them from causing damage and loss on critical assets. By injecting hunt software into system processes, security teams can hide their presence, thus mimicking the behavior of adversaries.

☑ Sensor hardening: No technology is infallible. If an adversary happens to discover the presence of a sensor, sensor hardening limits that adversary's ability to disable or otherwise reconfigure the sensor.

By using a stealthy hunt technology that offers all of these characteristics, an organization can trick adversaries into believing that no hunt sensors are present. This can cause adversaries to take fewer precautions and thus become easier to detect.

 TIP Organizations should look for hunt technologies designed with built-in stealth since it's extremely difficult for an organization to conceal noticeable hunt technologies from adversaries on its own.

Automation

The degree to which a hunt solution is automated can make a huge difference in the effectiveness and productivity of security analysts. Every action that hunt technologies can perform on behalf of a human hunter frees the hunter to execute the most impactful and challenging parts of the hunt, such as analyzing information provided by the hunt sensors, and expanding hunting to include other assets.

TIP Organizations should automate the hunt as much as possible by acquiring, deploying, and using hunt technologies. Organizations may also choose to develop scripts, software, and other supporting components to provide additional automation capabilities and to interface the hunt technologies with other functions and tools. See the "Enterprise Integration" section below for more information on this.

Workflow Support

A common problem of security software is poor workflow support. For example, a security analyst investigating an issue often has to access a separate console interface for each piece of software. This forces analysts to alternate between several consoles during a single investigation, creating significant inefficiencies and delaying analysis.

In contrast, a hunt solution can optimize hunters' efforts by streamlining workflow. A holistic hunt solution gives the hunter access to a wide range of information in a single console. This greatly reduces the time it takes for hunters to complete tasks, including deploying hunt sensors, analyzing hunt data, and evicting adversaries.

Enterprise Integration

Hunt solutions must provide robust integration with existing business processes and security infrastructure. An essential component of maximizing return on investment (ROI) for your hunt solution is to integrate it with the organization's existing security investments.

A great example of enterprise integration is the hunt solution providing information to the organization's SIEM. The hunt solution can instruct the SIEM to enforce remediation actions, from changing firewall rulesets to adding IPS signatures. Integration with the SIEM allows analysts to use hunt data when they look for potential security incidents. This integration also permits the SIEM to perform log management on behalf of the hunt solution.

Other examples of enterprise integration include:

- ☑ Using the organization's strategic priorities and risk assessment findings to prioritize hunting
- ☑ Interacting bi-directionally with existing incident management and ticket tracking solutions
- ☑ Directing operations tools to notify on-call personnel when their assistance is needed
- ☑ Leveraging sandboxes and other analysis technologies to automatically generate new indicators of compromise for use in hunting on other assets
- ☑ Accepting feeds from threat intelligence services to enable rapid hunting for known threats

To facilitate enterprise integration, look for a hunt solution that has open and well-documented APIs. Such APIs allow organizations to write their own integrations, integrate the hunt solution with their custom applications, and extend integration in the future with minimal effort.

Scalability

A final key attribute of a hunt solution is its scalability. When an organization is first adopting the hunt, scalability may not be a major concern, but as the value of hunting becomes obvious, its scope will naturally expand. This expansion is likely to be unmanageable and unsustainable unless the hunt solution can support all of the organization's IT assets and hunters.

Organizations should ensure that the hunt solution they acquire and deploy is not only sized reasonably for meeting current requirements, but also is easily expandable on an as-needed basis as requirements change.

For More Information on Endgame

Endgame's comprehensive hunt platform automates the hunt for advanced adversaries. Endgame enables hunters to identify known and never-before-seen adversaries in the enterprise environment by automating the Endgame hunt cycle. The Endgame hunt platform prevents compromises, and it detects and evicts adversaries before damage and loss can occur.

Endgame stands apart from other hunt technologies in many ways:

- It covers all phases of the hunt cycle, including securing the organization's assets.

- It offers continuous protection of the organization's assets through hunt sensors that detect and stop the use of attack techniques from advanced adversaries, including malware and other exploits that have never been seen before.

- It follows stealth principles to avoid adversaries detecting, manipulating, and evading the hunt sensors.

- It looks for malicious activity in all phases of the cyber kill chain so that compromises can be stopped well before damage occurs.

- It can stop and evict adversaries with precision, ensuring continuity of operations through any remediation actions.

For more information on how Endgame's solution can help your organization, visit https://www.endgame.com/our-platform, or read the "Think Offense: Automate the Hunt" white paper at http://pages.endgame.com/rs/627-YBU-612/images/ENDGAME%20-%20Think%20Offense%20-%20Automate%20The%20Hunt%20White%20Paper.pdf.

Glossary

adversary: An individual or group, such as a nation state, criminal organization, or hacktivist association, that poses a threat to an organization.

command and control (C&C): Communications between a compromised asset and an adversary-controlled system to enable an adversary to maintain a presence within the compromised asset.

cyber risk assessment report: A foundational document for all hunting efforts. It lists the organization's critical IT functions, grouping them by their relative priorities. The report also provides a threat assessment for the organization as a whole and for specific critical IT functions as appropriate. Hunters use the report as a source of information and prioritization guidance.

cyber kill chain: An attack executed in stages by an adversary, generally over an extended period of time, to go through an organization's systems and networks in order to eventually reach the sensitive data or services sought by the adversary. The concept of the cyber kill chain was first proposed by Lockheed Martin.

data science: The study of quantitative and computational methods for analyzing structured and unstructured data. Components of data science of particular importance to hunting include natural language processing (NLP) and machine learning techniques.

Detect: The third phase of the Endgame hunt cycle. It involves using hunt sensors' automated detection and data collection capabilities to find evidence of successful and failed attacks and identify adversaries by analyzing the collected data.

dwell time: The period during which an adversary maintains a continuous presence within an organization. This presence is generally achieved through malicious processes running on one or more assets.

enterprise integration: In the context of hunt technologies, the ability to have a hunt solution work with an organization's existing business processes and security infrastructure. Examples of enterprise integration include using the organization's strategic priorities and risk assessment findings to prioritize hunting, accepting feeds from threat intelligence services to enable rapid hunting for new known threats, and configuring the hunt platform to provide information to the organization's security information and event management (SIEM) solution.

hunt cycle: A series of phases that comprise the process of hunting. Endgame's hunt cycle phases are Survey, Secure, Detect, and Respond.

hunt platform: The heart of a centralized hunt automation solution for an enterprise. It automates several types of hunt tasks, including asset discovery and characterization, data collection, prevention, adversary detection, and remediation.

hunt policy: Documentation that contains all the requirements for hunting within the organization, without specifying step-by-step procedures or other low-level information. Hunt policies may also contain guidelines and recommendations. A hunt policy usually addresses hunting-related definitions, external requirements, personnel, hunt technology requirements, and metrics, at a minimum.

hunt sensor: Software installed on an asset to automate hunt actions within that asset, from data collection and attack prevention to adversary detection and remediation. An alternate approach to using the hunt sensor for security monitoring only is to use a sensorless monitoring method that relies on user mode and operating system data retrieved through an application programming interface (API). A sensorless approach can't provide continuous monitoring, so there are blind spots in the data.

hunt team: A group within an organization dedicated to hunting. The hunt team usually includes a team lead and several hunters. Larger teams may also contain hunt analysts, such as malware and forensic analysts.

hunter: An individual who hunts on behalf of an organization.

hunting: The process of proactively, stealthily, and methodically looking for signs of malicious activity within an organization's enterprise networks without prior knowledge of those signs, then ensuring that the malicious activity is removed from those networks and the systems connected to them.

indicators of compromise: Distinct characteristics corresponding to a particular attack campaign or piece of malware. Indicators of compromise are increasingly unique for each instance of an attack, making detection through known signatures unlikely or impossible.

insider threat: A threat posed by an adversary who is part of the organization, such as an employee. Many insider threats use some of the same tools and techniques that external adversaries use, so hunting can play an important role in detecting insider threats.

machine learning techniques: Computational techniques used by software to identify patterns and learn by processing and analyzing data. These techniques are a part of data science.

natural language processing (NLP) techniques: Techniques for analyzing unstructured text and extracting meaning from human languages. These techniques, which are a part of data science, can be adapted for application to malware code processing and analysis.

offense-based approach: A proactive approach to preventing breaches of critical data and defeating advanced adversaries. This takes place within the enterprise's networks. Hunting is an offense-based approach based on understanding adversaries' strategies and adopting their mindset when looking for signs of compromise within an organization.

persistence: The ability of an adversary to maintain access to a compromised asset even if the original entry points have been remediated so as to no longer be usable by the adversary.

Respond: The fourth phase of the Endgame hunt cycle. It involves stopping an attack by disrupting the adversary's access and preventing it from being regained, repairing damage to compromised assets, and informing the appropriate personnel of the actions taken by the hunters and the weaknesses that still need to be addressed.

rules of engagement: Documentation that specifies requirements for hunters' actions during all phases of the hunt cycle, as well as activities such as communications and reporting that are relevant across phases.

Secure: The second phase of the Endgame hunt cycle. It involves locking down monitored assets to ensure threats already in the environment are prevented from moving laterally and gaining further access. This phase also prevents execution of new malware and other exploits.

stealth: The ability to avoid detection. Adversaries use stealthy methods to conceal their actions and presence from organizations. Likewise, hunters rely on their hunt technologies functioning in an unobtrusive manner that's not readily identifiable by adversaries. Examples include operating covertly by hiding on disk and on the network, diversifying elements of hunt sensor software installed and operating on assets, and hardening sensor software to protect it from tampering.

Survey: The first phase of the Endgame hunt cycle. It involves discovering assets in the environment, determining which assets an adversary is most likely to target, and deploying sensors to monitor them and collect data on any malicious activity.